STRAY KIDS

Pure Magic

Alison James

sona BOOKS

© Danann Publishing Limited 2025

First published in the UK 2025 by Sona Books an imprint of Danann Publishing Ltd.

WARNING: For private domestic use only, any unauthorised copying, hiring, lending or public performance of this book is illegal.

CAT NO: SON0644

Photography courtesy of

Getty images:

Chung Sung-Jun	Taylor Hill	Elena Di Vincenzo	Jamie McCarthy
Mary Clavering	Kristy Sparow	Sergione Infuso	Josh Brasted
Johnny Louis	Julie Sebadelha	Dia Dipasupil	Barry Brecheisen
Santiago Felipe	Justin Shin	Michael Buckner	Rich Polk
Dave Benett	The Chosunilbo JNS	Gilbert Flores	JYP Entertainment
Roy Rochlin	Penske Media	Han Myung-Gu	Jung Yeon-je

Other images Alamy, Wiki Commons

Cover design Darren Grice at Ctrl-d
Book design concept Darren Grice at Ctrl-d
Layout design Samantha Richiardi
Proof Reader Ray Robb

All rights reserved. No Part of this title may be reproduced or transmitted in any material form (including photocopying or storing it in any medium by electronic means and whether or not transiently or incidentally to some other use of this publication) without the written permission of the copyright owner, except in accordance with the provisions of the Copyright, Designs and Patents Act 1988. Applications for the copyright owner's written permission should be addressed to the publisher.

This is an independent publication and it is unofficial and unauthorised and as such has no connection with Stray Kids or their management or any other organisation connected in any way whatsoever with the artist or artists featured in the book.

Printed in E.U.
ISBN: 978-1-917259-06-4

Contents

Introduction	10
Stray Kids... A History	18
Getting to Know... Bang Chan	30
Stray Kids in a K-pop universe	34
Getting to Know... Lee Know	44
Talk K-pop!	48
Getting to Know... Changbin	54
Speak Stray Kids	58
Getting to Know... Hyunjin	64
Discography	68
Getting to Know... Han	80
On the Road	84
Getting to Know... Felix	100
Awards	104
Getting to Know... Seungmin	110
Words of Wisdom	114
Getting to Know... I.N	130
Stray Kids... The Future	134

Getting to Know the
STRAY KIDS

Stray Kids live on stage at the I-Days
Milano Coca-Cola festival, Ippodromo
SNAI La Maura, Milan, 2024

INTRODUCTION

In the ever-evolving world of K-pop where countless groups rise and fall, Stray Kids have carved out a path entirely their own. From their humble beginnings as trainees at JYP Entertainment to becoming one of the most innovative forces in global music, Stray Kids represent more than just a boy band – they are a phenomenon. Their story is one of passion, resilience and unrelenting creativity, driven by a shared vision to make music that resonates deeply with their fans. Stray Kids' USP is their authenticity. Unlike many artists, they are not content to simply perform. They write, compose, and produce their own music, creating work which reflects their personal struggles, hopes and dreams, and emotions. The production unit 3RACHA – comprised of leader Bang Chan, Changbin, and Han – is the beating heart of the band, blending genres and sounds to create truly unique material. From hard-hitting anthems like 'God's Menu' to introspective tracks like 'Grow Up', their music mirrors the twists and turns, high and lows, and peaks and troughs of life.

Changbin, Seungmin, I.N, Felix, Han, Hyunjin, Lee Know and Bang Chan of Stray Kids pose at the American Music Awards 50th Anniversary in Los Angeles, 2024

11

INTRODUCTION

This beautifully presented book explores the journey of Stray Kids – from the high-stakes competition of their reality show debut to their meteoric rise as global superstars. Along the way, they have overcome setbacks – including personnel changes and the intense pressures of fame – to create music that speaks to millions. It is a testament to their resilience, teamwork, and the unwavering bond they share with their fans, known collectively as STAY. Stray Kids are more than just a band – they are a movement, inspiring a new generation to follow their own path. This is their story.

> Stray Kids bring the energy during a K-pop concert at Jamsil Stadium for Seoul Festa 2022 in Seoul, South Korea

Stray Kids perform at I-Days Milano Coca-Cola, Ippodromo SNAI La Maura in Milan, 2024

Stray Kids take the stage at the American Music Awards 50th Anniversary in Los Angeles, 2024

Stray Kids...
A HISTORY

"Do your thing, guys!"
JY Park, musician, producer, and founder of the K-pop phenomenon.

Right from the get-go in 2017, Stray Kids was unique compared to other K-pop productions. Rather than focusing on individual trainees competing against each other, JYP MUSIC decided the *Stray Kids* reality show would revolve around a pre-formed group working to prove they had what it took to debut together. JYP did not even define the band's name. The members conceptualised it themselves, the name originally referring to lost children wanting to chase their dreams and evolving to find a way out of the ordinary together.

Stray Kids' debut showcase as they hold their first performance in Seoul, 2018

Bang Chan of Stray Kids strikes a pose during a showcase for the group's fourth mini album, Cle 1: *Miroh*, in Seoul, 2019

The team was spearheaded by Bang Chan, a determined young trainee who had spent seven years preparing for his debut. Handpicked by JY Park himself to lead this new project, Bang Chan was tasked with assembling a group that would embody creativity, talent, and unity. He selected members he believed could not only excel individually, but also work seamlessly as team players. In addition to Bang Chan, the original lineup included Woojin, Lee Know, Changbin, Hyunjin, Han, Felix, Seungmin, and I.N. Together, they were tasked with showing the world what they could achieve under pressure.

Lee Know, Han, Changbin, Seungmin, Hyunjin, I.N, Woojin, Felix, and Bang Chan of Stray Kids stop by Build Studio in New York City on May 13, 2019

Stray Kids live at the 8th Gaon Chart K-Pop Awards in Seoul, 2019

Stray Kids, the reality show, first aired in late 2017, and showcased the intense challenges the group faced. Each episode was filled with tests of musical skill, dancing ability, teamwork, and resilience. The stakes were high – any member could be eliminated if they didn't meet JYP Entertainment's exacting standards. Early in the run, the group faced its first major setback when Felix and Lee Know were temporarily eliminated. This decision shocked both the members and the audience, highlighting as it did the ruthless reality of the K-pop industry. However, the boys' unwavering determination and the team's collective effort led to both members being reinstated by the end of the show. This moment of triumph became a defining feature of Stray Kids' identity as a group that stands together and fights for each other.

Before the show concluded, Stray Kids released their pre-debut single, 'Hellevator'. The track, written and produced by members of the group, was a raw, emotional depiction of their struggles as trainees. With its haunting melody, powerful rap verses, and heartfelt lyrics, 'Hellevator' quickly gained traction, drawing attention to the group even before their official debut. The song's success was a sign of things to come. Fans were captivated by Stray Kids' emotions and their willingness to address struggles that many idols often kept under wraps. This authenticity became a cornerstone of Stray Kids' identity.

After months of preparation, Stray Kids officially debuted on March 25, 2018, with the release of their first extended play, *I Am NOT*. The title track, 'District 9' showcased their signature sound – bold, rebellious, and infused with energy, a hybrid genre of hip-hop, rock and EDM with frenetic bass, sirens, aggressive raps, and hip-hop dance moves. Lyrically, the album introduced themes of self-discovery and individuality, resonating with listeners who felt out of place in society.

Their debut was met with critical acclaim, and their fanbase, STAY, began to take shape. The name 'STAY' itself reflected the group's desire to have their fans remain by their side throughout their journey.

From the start, Stray Kids set themselves apart by being heavily involved in their music production. Bang Chan, Changbin, and Han – the 3RACHA – were the driving force behind their experimental sound. After the release of the album *Go Live* on June 17, 2020, the public and some entertainment media outlets began calling Stray Kids the pioneers of 'mala taste music' – a name adopted from hot, spicy mala food seasoning. Their ability to write, compose, and produce tracks gave Stray Kids an edge in an industry where many groups rely on external producers. The themes in their early music, such as identity, struggle, and resilience, struck a chord with young listeners. Tracks like 'My Pace' and 'Grow Up' encouraged fans to embrace their individuality and persevere through life's challenges. From the very beginning, Stray Kids set themselves apart with their authenticity. Their music wasn't just about polished perfection – it was about raw emotions, real struggles, and the journey of self-discovery. They invited their audience to walk with them, not as idols on a pedestal, but as companions navigating life's uncertainties. Their beginnings shaped them into a group that values creativity, perseverance, and the power of standing together. This foundation laid the groundwork for their meteoric rise, transforming them from a scrappy survival show group into one of K-pop's most influential acts.

Cover art for I am NOT EP, released in 2018

Stray Kids' first significant breakthrough came with the release of 'Miroh' in 2019. The song, part of their *Clé 1: Miroh* album, showcased anthemic energy and complex choreography, earning them their first music show win. This milestone marked their arrival. However Stray Kids' journey to success hasn't been without hurdles. In 2019, Woojin, one of the original members, departed from the group for personal reasons. While this was a difficult moment, the remaining eight members rallied together, reaffirming their bond and commitment to their music and fans.

Stray Kids' early journey is a powerful reminder of how ambition, resilience, and teamwork can turn dreams into reality. Their start wasn't just the beginning of a group; it was the birth of a movement that would go on to inspire millions around the world.

Stray Kids A HISTORY

Stray Kids hit the stage for a showcase celebrating the release of their fourth mini album, CL 1: *Miroh*, in Seoul, 2019

Stray Kids pose at the Young Hollywood Studio in Los Angeles, California, 2019

Getting to Know... BANG CHAN

STRAY KIDS *Pure Magic*

"I don't want to be a leader who tells people what to do – I'd rather be a listener"

Getting to Know BANG CHAN

Bang Chan leads the 'Stray Kids'. He is the ultimate all-rounder, feted for his powerful vocals, exceptional dance ability, and his deep involvement in the production of the band's songs – plus he regularly writes, arranges Stray Kids' numbers and directs their music. As a leader, he's supportive and inspiring, always prioritising the well-being and growth of his members. Bang Chan's strong work ethic and passion for music have made him an influential figure in the K-pop scene. His leadership and dedication to his craft have earned him respect and admiration both within the K-pop industry and amongst fans worldwide. Fluent in English and Korean, and conversational in Japanese. Bang Chan is not just the leader of Stray Kids – he's the heart of the group. His role is pivotal to the band's music and group dynamic.

Bang Chan at Global Citizen Live in Central Park, New York City, 2023

Born Christopher Bang on October 3, 1997 in Sydney, Australia, he developed an early passion for music and dance – taking ballet and modern dance classes at Newtown High School of the Performing Arts. In 2010, aged 13, he passed a local audition in Australia for JYP Entertainment. Despite his young age, he moved to South Korea to train, joining JYPE in April 2011. Then known as Chris, he trained for several years. In late 2016, Bang Chan formed a hip-hop crew called '3RACHA' with trainees Han Ji-sung ('J.One') and Seo Chang-bin ('SPEARB'), as part of which he adopted the tag 'CB97'. Throughout 2017, the trio uploaded self-composed mixtapes and extended plays to SoundCloud. Bang Chan's individual picture and name were officially revealed by JYPE in October 2017 ahead of his inclusion in the Stray Kids show. He was introduced with the roles 'Producing', 'Vocal', 'Rap', and 'Dance' in addition to being the leader of the 'Male Group Project' he formed by himself with J.Y. Park. On the final episode of the show in December 2017, it was confirmed that Bang Chan would debut as the leader of Stray Kids. In March 2018, he debuted with the mini album *I am NOT* as the leader, the producer, and a rapper. In March 2020, he released a dance cover of 'My House' by 2PM, as part of the SKZ-PLAYER series. Two months later, Bang Chan released the self-composed song 'I Hate to Admit'. Other solo, self-penned releases include 'Connected' from late 2022. Until 2023, he broadcast live streams, entitled 'Chan's Room', on VLive and YouTube. The same year, he was promoted as a regular member of the Korean Music and Copyright Association, or KOMCA. In October 2024, he donated 100 million won (approximately $70,000) to the 'Community Chest of Korea' to help people with developmental disabilities. He was then appointed as a member of the 'Honour Society'.

Bang Chan attends the Fendi Spring/Summer 2025 runway show during Milan Fashion Week, Italy, 2024

Getting to Know BANG CHAN

Charismatic Bang Chan has the warmest smile, complete with dimples! Like the rest of the Kids, he loves to experiment with hair styles and colours. From natural black to blonde, silver, and pastel shades, he's not afraid to try bold hues. His hair styles vary from slicked-back looks and fluffy perms, to straight fringes. Every look seems to suit him. BC is 171cm (5'7") tall, has great posture, and is fit and toned with broad shoulders and a slim waist. When it comes to fashion, Bang Chan is known for his streetwear-inspired looks, often combining casual and edgy styles, reflecting his laid-back yet fashion-forward vibe. He's often seen wearing accessories like necklaces, rings, and caps, which personalise his look. Bang Chan's visuals exude a magical mix of boy-next-door charm and the confidence of a leader – making him approachable yet awe-inspiring at the same time. His look sums him up – friendly, hardworking, and effortlessly cool.

FUN FACT FILE

- **SK** Fans often call him 'Chan' or 'Channie', while other Stray Kids members affectionately call him Chris.
- **SK** Before focusing on music, he was an active swimmer, and even competed at a national level during his youth.
- **SK** He loves chicken and doesn't shy away from trying different cuisines, though he has mentioned he can't handle spicy food.
- **SK** His favourite artists and inspirations include Drake, Justin Bieber, and DAY6.
- **SK** His star sign is Libra.

'Never ones to follow trends, Stray Kids exist in their own arena where their only competition is themselves'

New Musical Express

Stray Kids light up the stage during their District 9: *Unlock World Tour* at the Watsco Center in Miami, Florida, 2020

Since their formation, Stray Kids have achieved remarkable global success, positioning themselves among the very top K-pop groups. Their accomplishments include multiple number-one albums on the Billboard 200, significant album sales, and international recognition. Notably, they became the first K-pop group to debut at number one on the Billboard 200 with their first five chart entries. The eight-piece holds a uniquely powerful position in K-pop as trailblazers of the fourth generation of idol groups.

Stray Kids perform for a showcase celebrating the release of their fourth mini album, CL 1: *Miroh*, in Seoul, 2019

Stray Kids during the District 9: *Unlock World Tour* at the Watsco Center in Miami, Florida, 2020

Other 'fourth gen' groups such as ATEEZ, TXT, and ITZY have enjoyed considerable success, but Stray Kids are in a different league. With their emphasis on self-production, creative freedom, and bold experimentation in music and performance, they have redefined what it means to be a K-pop idol group. As a band that writes, produces, and choreographs its own original music, Stray Kids stand out as one of the few K-pop acts taking full creative control of their artistry. They are K-pop pioneers with their production unit, 3RACHA (Bang Chan, Changbin, and Han), setting a benchmark for idols wanting to take charge of their sound, look, and material. They're also genre-blenders, with Stray Kids music incorporating EDM, hip-hop, rock, and rap. Their body of work ranges from hard hitting tracks like 'God's Menu' and 'Thunderous', to heart-felt anthems like 'Grow Up' and 'My Pace'.

Standing Tall! STRAY KIDS IN A K-POP UNIVERSE

Fans wave their "Wolf Chan" SKZOO plushies in the crowd during the Global Citizen Festival at Central Park, New York City, 2023

Stray Kids are famed for high-octane performances that leave audiences breathless. Their live shows are a mix of impeccable choreography, powerful vocals, and charismatic stage presence. Whether performing at a sold-out Tokyo Dome or headlining a global festival like Lollapalooza, Stray Kids deliver an unforgettable experience that more than justifies their reputation as global superstars. In addition to their performances, they have embraced technology to enhance fan engagement – virtual concerts, immersive music videos, and creative use of social media platforms like TikTok have allowed them to reach and interact with fans in innovative ways. They are at the forefront of integrating the digital world with music, setting new trends in fan experiences. Stray Kids' success is inseparable from their devoted fanbase, known as STAY. This fandom is one of the most passionate and diverse in K-pop, encompassing millions of fans worldwide. The group's genuine connection with STAYs is evident in their interactions, whether through heartfelt messages during concerts or regular live streams where the boys share personal thoughts and jokes. This bond is more than just regular artist-fan interaction – it's a partnership. STAY actively participate in the group's success, from streaming their music to trending hashtags in support of the group. Stray Kids, in return, often dedicate songs and performances to their fans, making STAY a truly integral part of who they are.

The group represent more than just music – they are regarded as a symbol of resilience and authenticity. Their group name embodies their journey as 'kids' who are finding their way in life, and they invite their fans to join them. STAY are more than happy to. They relate to Stray Kids and see the group as role models who encourage individuality and self-expression. However the eight-piece reaches a wider cultural sphere. Stray Kids incorporate elements of Korean heritage into their music and performances, as heard in tracks like 'Thunderous' which blend traditional sounds with modern beats. By doing so, Korean culture is introduced to a global audience in a fresh and exciting way. Stray Kids aren't just idols in South Korea, either. Their popularity spans across Asia, the Americas, Europe, and beyond – the 'Manic World Tour' (2022/23) and 'dominATE World Tour' (2024/25) have sold out across the globe. A feat accomplished by few K-pop groups. Their influence also extends beyond music. Members like Hyunjin and Felix have become fashion icons, collaborating with luxury brands such as Valentino and Louis Vuitton. Involvement in high-profile events like Paris Fashion Week further elevates their global profile, positioning them as world ambassadors of K-pop.

Stray Kids' position in K-pop is not just about their present achievements but also their role as trailblazers for future generations. They have redefined what it means to be an idol, emphasizing creativity, hard work, and genuine connection. Their success proves that self-produced music and a fearless approach can resonate on a global scale. As they continue to grow, Stray Kids are likely to influence the trajectory of K-pop, inspiring new artists to take creative risks and forge deeper connections with their fans. They are not merely following the path set by their predecessors, they are carving a new one, ensuring their legacy as one of the most influential groups in the history of K-pop.

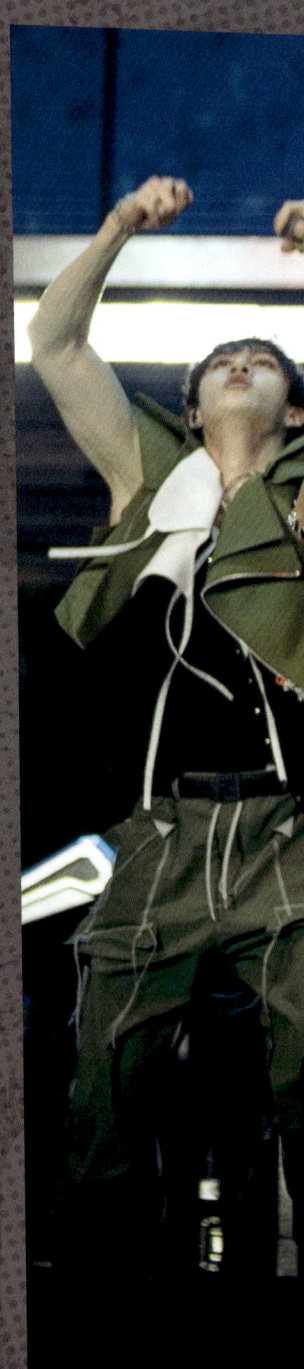

Stray Kids are more than just leaders of the fourth generation; they are a **revolutionary force**, a group that embodies the evolution of K-pop into a global cultural phenomenon. Their journey is a testament to their talent, hard work, and unwavering connection to their fans, ensuring their place at the forefront of K-pop for years to come.

Stray Kids perform at I-Days Milano Coca-Cola, Ippodromo SNAI La Maura in Milan, 2024

Standing Tall: STRAY KIDS IN A K-POP UNIVERSE

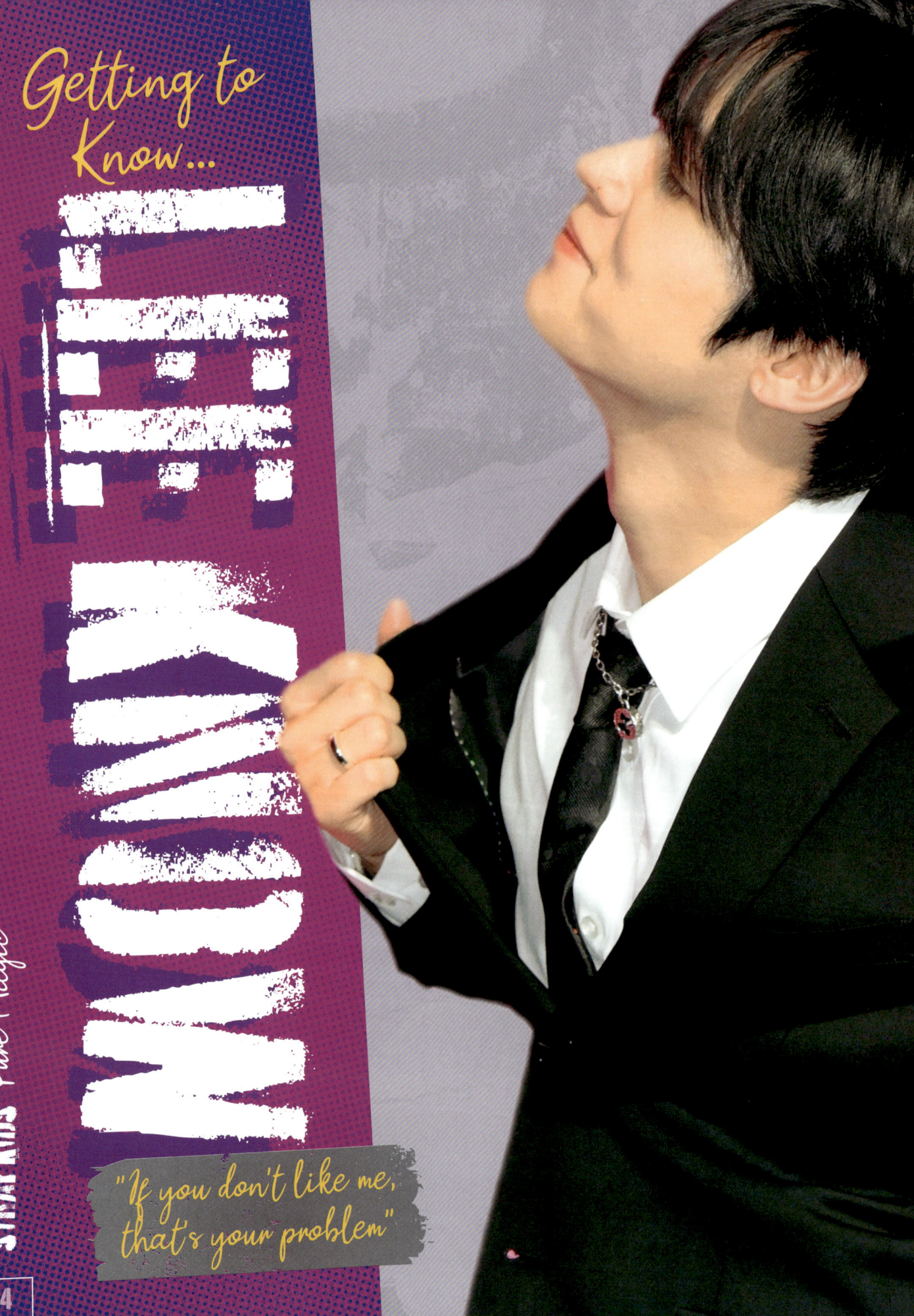

STRAY KIDS Pure Magic

Getting to Know...

LEE KNOW

"If you don't like me, that's your problem"

Lee Know is one of the most charismatic and multi-talented members of Stray Kids. He is celebrated for his exceptional dance skills, charismatic stage presence, and versatile talent. Widely recognised as one of Stray Kids' main dancers, and key vocalist, he plays a big role in choreographing and executing the group's dynamic and powerful routines. Known for his sharp and precise movements and his speciality – hip-hop, he consistently earns praise for his technical skill and artistry. He is also loved for his multifaceted personality. Onstage, he captivates fans with his intensity, while offstage he charms with his quirky sense of humour, love of cats, and warm yet mischievous aura. He particularly loves and cares for Stray Kids' fans, earning him a dedicated following.

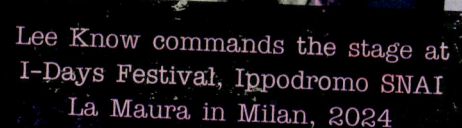

Lee Know commands the stage at I-Days Festival, Ippodromo SNAI La Maura in Milan, 2024

Born Lee Minho on October 25 1998 in Gimpo, South Korea, he started dancing in middle school. He joined the hip-hop crew 'Cupcakes' at Souldance Studio in Seoul, and stayed there for five years. With them, he participated in various dance competitions such as 'World of Dance' in 2016. He was a backup dancer for BTS from 2016 to 2017, but wanted to be in the spotlight. Lee had auditioned for JYP Entertainment in 2015, but wasn't called back for two years. He became a trainee on July 15, 2017, making him the member of the group with the shortest training period. He is famous for learning the agency's 40 basic dance steps in two weeks, a record previously held by TWICE's Momo, who took three months. Lee participated in JYPE's 'Homecoming" trainee showcase in August 2017, teaming up with other future members of *Stray Kids*. Due to their strong collective performance, all were selected to debut in the agency's next boy group, and he subsequently participated in the survival show Stray Kids. Although eliminated in episode four he rejoined the show in episode nine due to fan voting and popular demand. Lee Know has a certain duality – he's a playful and quirky personality offstage but transforms into a fierce performer when onstage.

FUN FACT FILE

- **SK** He's a cat person and has three kitties – Soonie, Doongie and Dori. He jokingly calls himself a cat due to his feline-like features and mannerisms.
- **SK** He's skilled in martial arts and enjoys showcasing his flexibility and strength.
- **SK** He describes himself as weird, but in a cute way and often refers to himself in the third person.
- **SK** He has over 10 nicknames including Minho, Catboy, Choco Prince, Mandu (Korean for dumpling) and Lino.
- **SK** His star sign is Scorpio.

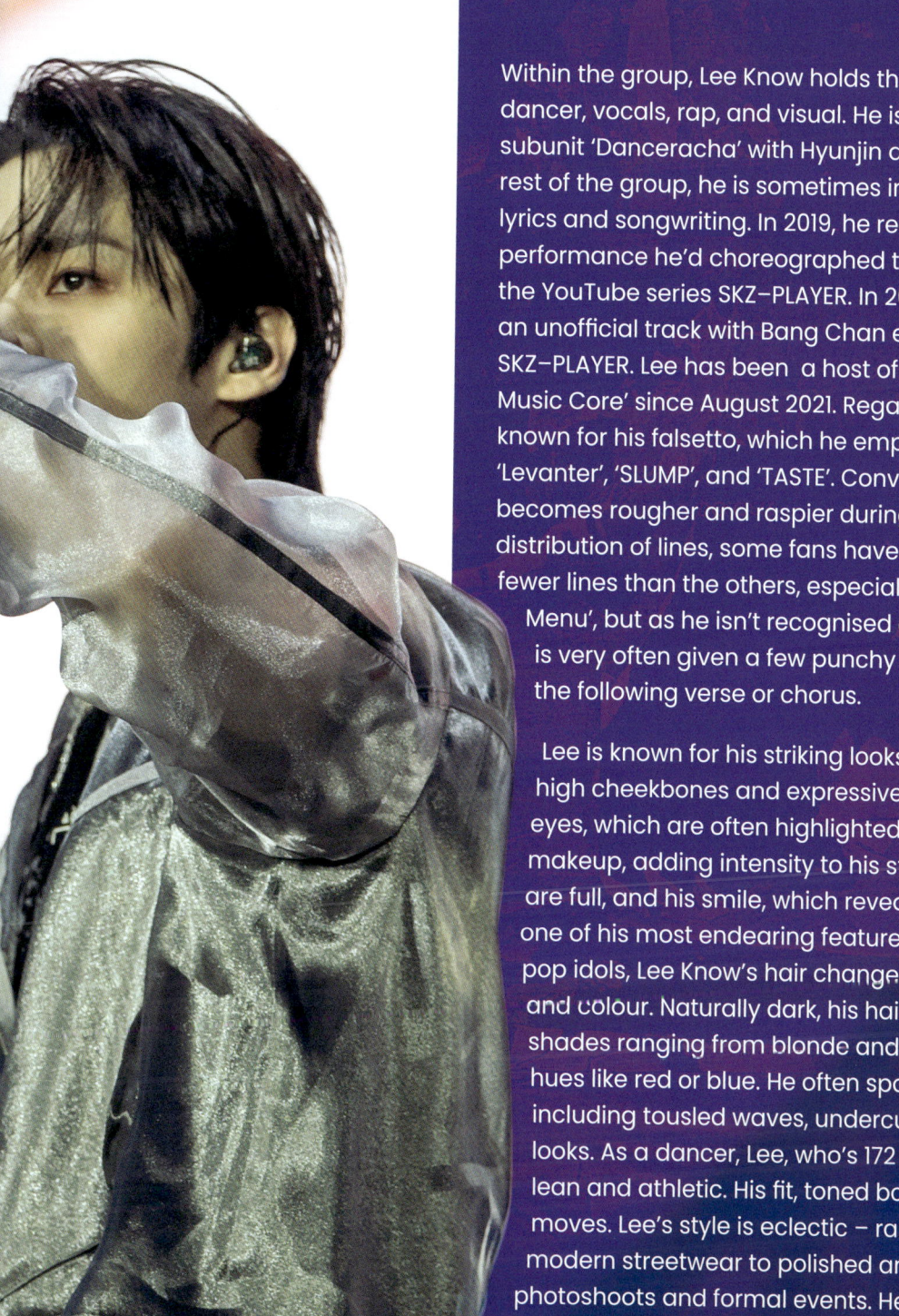

Getting to Know LEE KNOW

Within the group, Lee Know holds the positions of main dancer, vocals, rap, and visual. He is part of the unofficial subunit 'Danceracha' with Hyunjin and Felix. Like the rest of the group, he is sometimes involved directly with lyrics and songwriting. In 2019, he released a dance performance he'd choreographed titled 'DAWN' via the YouTube series SKZ–PLAYER. In 2021, he released an unofficial track with Bang Chan entitled 'Drive' on SKZ–PLAYER. Lee has been a host of the show 'Show! Music Core' since August 2021. Regarding singing, he is known for his falsetto, which he employs in the songs 'Levanter', 'SLUMP', and 'TASTE'. Conversely, his voice becomes rougher and raspier during the rap parts. In the distribution of lines, some fans have noted that he has fewer lines than the others, especially in the song 'God's Menu', but as he isn't recognised as a lead rapper, he is very often given a few punchy words that cut into the following verse or chorus.

Lee is known for his striking looks. He is blessed with high cheekbones and expressive almond-shaped eyes, which are often highlighted with smoky or subtle makeup, adding intensity to his stage look. His lips are full, and his smile, which reveals his dimples, is one of his most endearing features. As with many K-pop idols, Lee Know's hair changes frequently in style and colour. Naturally dark, his hair has been dyed in shades ranging from blonde and ash grey to bold hues like red or blue. He often sports trendy hairstyles, including tousled waves, undercuts, or straight, sleek looks. As a dancer, Lee, who's 172 cm (5'8") in height, is lean and athletic. His fit, toned body complements his moves. Lee's style is eclectic – ranging from edgy and modern streetwear to polished and elegant outfits for photoshoots and formal events. He likes experimenting with layering, accessories, and bold outfits. Sophisticated yet playful, charismatic yet approachable. . . that's Lee Know. He is an integral member of the Stray Kids family.

Lee Know at I-Days Festival, Ippodromo SNAI La Maura in Milan, 2024

TALK K-POP!
It has a language all of its own...

Lee Know and Hyunjin at the 2024 SBS Gayo Daejeon red carpet, Incheon, South Korea

TALK K-POP! It has a language all of its own...

Aegyo (애교): Acting cute or adorable, often demonstrated through gestures, expressions, or tone of voice.

All-kill: When a song tops all major Korean music charts simultaneously.

Bias: Your favourite member of a K-pop group.

Bias Wrecker: The member who tempts you to stray from your bias.

B-Side: Non-title tracks on an album, often fan favourites.

Comeback: A group's return with a new album or single, often accompanied by a fresh concept.

Concept: The theme or style of an album or song, encompassing visuals, music, and performance.

Daesang (대상): A prestigious award given to the best artist, album, or song at a major awards show.

Debut: A group or artist's first official release and promotion.

Ending Fairy: The member who gets a close-up shot at the end of a performance, striking a dramatic or cute pose.

Fan Chant: A coordinated cheer or chant by fans during a performance, usually including member names or key lyrics.

Fan Service: Gestures by idols to please fans – like making heart signs, waving, or sharing personal stories.

Golden Maknae (황금 막내): A term for A group's youngest member (maknae) who excels at many things.

Group Visual: The member considered the most conventionally attractive or representative of the group's image.

Hiatus: A temporary break in promotions or activities, often for rest or personal reasons.

Hallyu (한류): The 'Korean Wave', referring to the global popularity of Korean culture, including K-pop.

Idol: A K-pop artist, typically trained by entertainment agencies for years before debuting.

It Boy/It Girl: A member or solo artist known for their universal appeal and influence.

J-Line: Japanese members of a group.

Killing Part: The most memorable or impactful part of a song or choreography.

Leader: The member responsible for leading and representing the group.

Lightstick: A customized, often glowing device fans use at concerts to show support for their group.

Maknae (막내): The youngest member of a group.

MV: Music video.

Netizens (네티즌): Internet users, particularly those discussing K-pop and Korean culture.

Official Colours: Colours chosen to represent a group or fandom.

OT#: Supporting all members of a group, e.g. OT8 for Stray Kids.

Position: A member's role in the group (e.g., main vocal, lead dancer, rapper).

Pre-debut: The period before a group or artist officially debuts.

TALK K-POP! It has a language all of its own...

I.N of Stray Kids performs for I-Days at Ippodromo SNAI La Maura in Milan, 2024

STRAY KIDS *Pure Magic*

52

Maxident Mini Album photobook

TALK K-POP! It has a language all of its own...

Rookie: A newly debuted artist or group, typically in their first year.

Repackaged Album: A re-release of an album with additional songs or a new concept.

Selca: A self-taken photo or selfie.

Sasaeng: An obsessive fan who invades idols' privacy.

Sub-unit: A smaller group formed from a larger group, often with a different musical style.

Title Track: The main song promoted from an album, often with a music video.

Trainee: Someone undergoing training to become a K-pop idol.

Live: A popular streaming platform where idols interact with fans.

Win: When a song wins first place on a Korean music show.

Whale: A big-spending fan who supports idols by buying large quantities of merchandise.

Yeonjung (연정): Friendships or bonds between members, often celebrated by fans.

Zombie Streaming: When fans stream a song on repeat to artificially boost its chart performance.

Getting to Know...

CHANGBIN

STRAY KIDS *Pure Magic*

"I may look tough but I'm really soft like mochi"

Getting to Know CHANGBIN

Changbin's creative genius and vibrant personality are central to Stray Kids' identity. His contributions to their music and his ability to switch between playful and intense make him a beloved member of the group and a firm fan favourite. One of the fastest rappers in Korea – and named by *Briefly* magazine in 2024 as the 17th in the world– with a top speed of 11.13 syllables per second, Changbin's rap is instantly recognizable for its scratchy feeling and intensity. His voice can switch from a deep, husky tone to a nasal high pitched tone, giving a rough feeling. He is known for having a very loud voice which can be heard easily, even without a microphone. Known for his fast-paced, aggressive rap style, Changbin is one of the group's strongest rappers and often delivers the most intense verses in their tracks. Apart from rap, he occasionally showcases his vocal skills and emotional range in the group's ballads and slower tracks. His performance aspects include coolness, charisma, and darkness. Changbin is one of the most dynamic and talented members of Stray Kids. As a core member of 3RACHA, Changbin has co-written and co-produced most of Stray Kids' music, contributing significantly to their signature sound.

Changbin live on stage during the Global Citizen Festival at Central Park, New York, 2023

Seo Chang-bin was born on August 11 1999 in Yongin and raised in Uiwang and Seoul, South Korea. He wanted to become a singer because when he danced and rapped at his school's festival, the audience's reaction was unforgettable. In 2016, Changbin joined JYP Entertainment through an audition with a self-composed rap song. He formed a hip-hop crew called '3RACHA' with fellow trainees Bang Chan ('CB97') and Han Ji-sung ('J.One') where he adopted the stage name 'SPEARB'. They uploaded self-composed extended plays on SoundCloud throughout 2017. Changbin's individual picture and name were officially revealed by the company in October 2017 ahead of his participation in the upcoming survival show Stray Kids. He was introduced with the roles 'Producer' and 'Rap'. On the final episode of the show in December 2017, it was confirmed that Changbin would debut with the boy group Stray Kids. In March 2018, Changbin debuted with the mini album *I am NOT* as a lead rapper and producer of Stray Kids. In May 2020, he released the self-composed song 'Streetlight' featuring Leader Bang Chan as part of the SKZ-PLAYER series. Later that year, he released another self-composed number 'Cypher'.

In December 2022, Changbin wrote and composed his original solo song 'DOODLE' for the compilation album *SKZ-REPLAY*. The next September, he released the song 'Fly-High', composed and sung by himself, as part of a campaign for the Samsung Galaxy Z Flip 5. In February 2024, he released the remake song '8th grader (Respect your dreams)' with South Korean singer Kim Chang-wan as part of the campaign for the Samsung Galaxy S24. In October 2024, Changbin featured on the track 'VAY' of ITZY's ninth mini album *GOLD*, for which he was in charge of writing and composition.

Changbin attends the Ferragamo 23 Pre-Fall Collection Pop-up Store in Seoul, 2023

Changbin has revolutionised his body over the years. Skinny when he debuted, he has since bulked up by working out. These days he is widely recognized for his muscular and athletic physique, often jokingly referred to as having 'bodybuilder energy' among fans. He is dedicated to fitness and regularly working out, and this makes him stand out as one of the more muscular idols in K-pop. Changbin's style reflects his confident and charismatic personality, blending streetwear with edgy aesthetics. He frequently wears oversized hoodies, graphic tees, cargo trousers, and sneakers, embodying a casual yet trendy vibe. For performances, his style takes on a more intense and polished edge, with tailored outfits, leather jackets, or statement pieces that match his fiery rap persona.

FUN FACT FILE

- His several nicknames include 'Binsual' – a combination of Changbin and visual, 'Binnie', 'Baby Changbin', 'Lewis' – his English name chosen by the members, 'Binderella'' – because he does chores around the house, and 'Dark Bunny', which is a playful nod to his love of dark aesthetics combined with his cute side.

- He often makes chicken breast shakes.

- He can impersonate Spongebob.

- He can't sleep without his Munchlax plush toy, which he calls Gyu.

- His star sign is Leo.

Getting to Know CHANGBIN

SPEAK STRAY KIDS

When you know you know...

STRAY KIDS *Pure Magic*

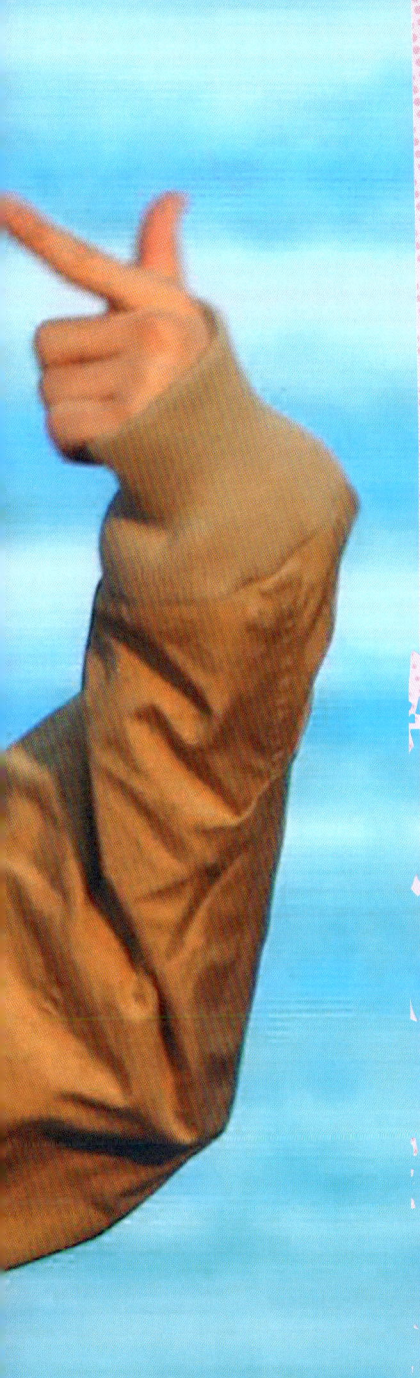

Aussie Line: Bang Chan and Felix – both are from Australia.

Awkward Silence: A playful phrase and song title from their early discography, often referenced in SK's humour.

Bang Chan: Leader of Stray Kids, often called Chan, Chris, or Channie.

Baby Bread: A nickname for I.N (Jeongin), the youngest member, for his adorable and youthful vibes.

Best Leader: A common term used by STAYs to describe Bang Chan due to his exceptional care for the members.

Chan's Room: A regular live stream hosted by Bang Chan where he chatted with fans, shared music, and gave advice. Bring it back!

Cheese: A playful, high-energy Stray Kids song that highlights their humour and individuality.

Double Knot: A Stray Kids track symbolizing determination and freedom, often performed with powerful choreography.

Felix: Known for his deep voice, freckles, and baking talents. Nicknames include Lixie and Sunshine.

Fox: Han Jisung is often compared to a fox for his sharp, playful features and personality.

Felix live on stage at the British Summer Time festival in Hyde Park, London, 2024

God's Menu:	One of Stray Kids' most iconic tracks, known for its impactful 'du–du–du–du' sound and hard-hitting choreography.
Hyunjin:	Known as the group's Visual King and a talented dancer, often referred to as Prince Hwang for his regal visuals.
I.N (Jeongin):	The group's maknae, often called Baby Bread or Yokshim Maknae (determined youngest).
Jisung (Han):	Known for his exceptional rap and vocal abilities, as well as his comedic timing and songwriting skills.
Kingdom:	A survival show Stray Kids participated in and won in 2021, showcasing their creative stage performances.
Lee Know:	Stray Kids' lead dancer and known for his love of cats. Nicknames include Minho or Minmin.
Lee know's Cats:	Soonie, Dori, and Doongie – the cats that Minho adores and often talks about.
Maknae Line:	Refers to the youngest members – Hyunjin, Felix, Seungmin, and I.N.
Maniac:	A popular Stray Kids title track from their album *ODDINARY*, known for its 'thunderous' impact.
Noeasy:	Stray Kids' second full album, known for its creative promotion campaign that played on the title's pun ('noisy').
Nine or None:	A phrase that signifies the group's commitment to staying together, referencing their strong bond.

Hyunjin takes the stage during Day One of the Lollapalooza Festival in Paris, 2023

Racha Units:	Stray Kids have three subunits – 3RACHA: Bang Chan, Han, and Changbin, the primary producers and songwriters; DanceRacha: Lee Know, Hyunjin, and Felix, focusing on choreography, VocalRacha, Seungmin and I.N, emphasizing vocals.
STAY:	The name of Stray Kids' fandom, derived from the idea of 'Stay with Stray Kids'.
Seungmin:	Known as the group's Golden Voice, often nicknamed Puppy for his resemblance to one.
SKZ-Player:	Stray Kids' platform for releasing self-produced songs or covers that aren't part of official albums.
SKZ-Record:	A platform for members to share raw, emotional tracks or demos.
Thunderous:	A high-energy Stray Kids title track symbolizing boldness and self-confidence.
Tiny Chan:	Bang Chan's tiny, cartoonish representation often used in memes and artwork.
Wolfgang:	A performance track Stray Kids created for Kingdom, showcasing their wild, untamed energy.
Yongbok:	Felix's Korean name, often used affectionately by the members and fans.
Zone:	A song from *MAXIDENT* that explores themes of self-discovery and individuality.

Hyunjin performs at I-Days Festival, Ippodromo SNAI La Maura, Milan, 2024

Getting to Know... HYUNJIN

STRAY KIDS *Pure Magic*

"When I dance, I feel free, like I'm painting with my body"

Striking visuals, charismatic stage presence and exceptional dancing skills... Hyunjin is one talented 'namja-ae'. Musical and performance talents aside, Hyunjin is also admired for his passion for art and self-expression, often sharing his personal artworks with fans. With his multifaceted talents and warm personality, Hyunjin has established himself as a prominent figure in the global K-pop scene, inspiring fans worldwide. He is a standout performer, known for his expressive and sharp moves, with his dance covers regularly receiving widespread praise. A very popular dancer and prominent during key moments of choreographies, Hyunjin assumes the role of Center within the group.

Hyunjin live at the Lollapalooza Festival, Hippodrome de Longchamp in Paris, 2023

Getting to Know HYUNJIN

Hyunjin, full name Hwang Hyunjin, was born on March 20, 2000 in Seoul, South Korea. As a child, he spent several months in Las Vegas, where he used the first name Sam. Back in Seoul, Hyunjin was shopping with his mother when a casting director from JYP Entertainment spotted him and offered him an audition at the agency. Before becoming a trainee, he had never danced or rapped. Hyunjin joined JYPE in 2015. As a trainee, he became interested in dance while watching the agency's seniors perform on stage. He then joined the School of Performing Arts (SOPA), an arts high school often chosen by idols, to learn choreography. He studied contemporary dance and hip-hop. In August 2017, Hyunjin took part in JYPE's trainee showcase 'Homecoming' where he teamed up with other future members of Stray Kids. Due to their strong performance, they were selected to debut in the agency's next boy group. In October 2017, he was officially revealed as a participant in

FUN FACT FILE

- **SK** His nicknames are 'Prince', due to his regal visuals, 'Jinnie', and 'Our Lovely Bread' because of his soft features and loveable personality.
- **SK** He has a meticulous skincare routine, which explains his flawless complexion.
- **SK** His hobbies include drawing, writing in his diary, and discovering new music.
- **SK** His favourite colours are black and white because they match his classic and clean style.
- **SK** His star sign is Pisces.

the idol show Stray Kids, and at the end of the series it was revealed that he would indeed join the group. In March 2018, Hyunjin officially debuted in Stray Kids with the mini album *I am NOT*, serving as one of the main dancers alongside Lee Know, and a secondary rapper. He graduated from the School of Performing Arts (SOPA) in February 2019, having majored in dance, and went on to form the sub-unit 'Danceracha' with fellow Stray Kids members Lee Know and Felix. Hyunjin presented the Korean TV show 'Show! Music Core' from February 2019 to February 2021. In December 2019, he joined KBS's project group 'BBANGBBANGZ' with Yoon Sanha, Choi Bomin, and Lee Daewhi, bringing together idols born in 2000 for special performances. In May 2020, he released a dance performance he choreographed to Billie Eillish's song 'When the Party's Over', and released the original song 'Miss You' several months later. In February 2021, he became the subject of controversy after being accused of bullying while at school. He wrote a public apology letter and took time out. His appearance in the music video for the single 'Mixtape: OH' in June 2021 marked his comeback. That July he released a dance performance he choreographed to Sam Tinnesz's song 'Play with Fire'. Three months later, he was chosen as Artist of the Month by the STUDIO CHOOM channel for a special performance. In August 13 2022, he released the song 'Ice Cream'. In July 2023, Hyunjin became a global ambassador for Versace – the first K-pop artist to be named as an ambassador for the brand.

Hyunjin is heavily associated with performance within the group. His dance style is notable for its dramatics, use of facial expressions, and an alternation between sharp and loose movements. This is highlighted in the chorus of 'Back Door' and his dance practice to Taemin's 'Criminal'. When it comes to rapping, over time he has emerged as a 'lazy rapper' and his style can be heard in 'Muddy Water' or 'VENOM'. In contrast, he sometimes has short parts with percussive inflections marking the rhythm, as in 'God's Menu' or 'CIRCUS'.

Sartorially speaking, almond-eyed, full-lipped Hyunjin oscillates between chic and classy in blazers and tailored suits, and streetwear cool in hoodies, trendy sneakers, and bold accessories. Elegant and ethereal, he is often likened to a modern prince due to his tall stature and graceful demeanour. Hyunjin is regarded as one of the group's trendsetters. Like his Stray Kids 'brothers', he frequently experiments with hair colours and styles, ranging from natural black or brown to bold shades like blonde, pink, or red. He frequently goes blonde for comebacks. His hairstyles often shift between long, flowing locks – which enhance his princely look – to shorter, edgy cuts that highlight his fine features.

Hyunjin at the Versace Women's Fashion, Autumn Winter, Milan, Italy, 2024

Stray Kids...
DISCOGRAPHY

Stray Kids' music is – and always has been – characterised by bold experimentation, self–expression, and themes of growth, resilience, and individuality. From rebellious anthems to heartfelt ballads, their discography offers a diverse soundscape that resonates with fans worldwide.

Singles

Hellevator OCTOBER 17 2017
Pre-debut single that introduced their distinct style.

Astronaut NOVEMBER 14 2019
A gift to fans during a transitional period.

Christmas EveL NOVEMBER 29 2021
A festive single with a playful twist.

Mixtape Projects.
Series of tracks like 'Oh', 'Gone Days', and 'On Track' released as standalone projects.

Stray Kids perform at the 2023 Billboard Music Awards in Seoul

STRAY KIDS *Pure Magic*

Stray Kids hold debut showcase in Seoul, Korea on 24th March, 2018

Mini Albums (EPs)

I Am NOT MARCH 26 2018
Title track 'District 9'. Debut EP with themes of self-discovery.

I Am WHO AUGUST 6 2018
Title track 'My Pace'. Focused on individuality and personal growth.

I Am YOU OCTOBER 22 2018
Title track 'I Am YOU. Explores connection and unity.

Clé 1: Miroh MARCH 25 2019
Title track 'Miroh'. Their first music show win.

Clé 2: Yellow Wood JUNE 19 2019
Title tracks 'Side Effects' and 'TMT'. Includes 'Mixtape' tracks showcasing their versatility.

Clé: Levanter DECEMBER 9 2019
Title track 'Levanter'. Marked a transitional period for the group.

Oddinary MARCH 18 2022
Title track 'Maniac'. First No. 1 on the Billboard 200.

Maxident OCTOBER 7 2022
Title track 'CASE 143'. Combines romance themes with their signature sound.

Rock-Star NOVEMBER 10 2023
Title track 'Lalalala'. Showcases a rock-inspired concept.

Ate JULY 19 2024
Title track 'Chk Chk Boom', highlighting the group's versatility.

Stray Kids... DISCOGRAPHY

Maxident Mini Album Photobook

A billboard of Stray Kids in the Shibuya shopping district in Tokyo, Japan

Studio Albums

GO生 (GO) JUNE 17 2020
Title track 'God's Menu'. First full-length album, showcasing a dynamic mix of genres.

Noeasy AUGUST 23 2021
Title track 'Thunderous'. Known for its powerful energy and traditional Korean influences.

5-Star JUNE 2 2023
Title track 'S-Class'. Achieved massive success, becoming one of their best-selling albums globally.

The Sound FEBRUARY 22 2023
Title track 'The Sound'. Stray Kids' first Japanese studio album.

Giant NOVEMBER 13 2024
Stray Kids' second Japanese studio album, including singles 'Night' and 'Falling Up'. Both tracks served as themes for season two of the anime 'Tower of God'.

HOP (SKZHIP HIPTAPE) DECEMBER 13 2024
Mixtape, marketed as 'SKZHIP HIPTAPE', blending hip-hop influences and introducing the 'SKZHIP' genre, a fusion of the group's initials and hip hop. Features solo tracks from each of the eight.

Repackaged Albums

IN生 (IN LIFE) SEPTEMBER 14 2020
Repackage of 'GO LIVE', featuring additional tracks

Seungmin at a Chanel Pop-Up Event, Seoul, 2024

STRAY KIDS *Pure Magic*

like 'Back Door'.

Compilation Albums

SKZ2020 MARCH 18 2020
re-recorded tracks from their discography with updated vocals following Woojin's departure.

Original Soundtracks (OSTs) and Collaborations

'Top' and 'Slump' 2020
OSTs for the anime 'Tower of God'. 'Top' was also released as a single in Japan.

Here Always (Seungmin) 2021
OST for 'Hometown Cha-Cha-Cha'.

Why APRIL 12 2024
This Japanese single served as the theme song for the television drama 'Re: Revenge – Yokubo no Hate ni'.

Lose My Breath – featuring Charlie Puth MAY 10 2024
A collaborative digital single blending Stray Kids' dynamic style with Charlie Puth's signature sound.

SLASH JULY 2024
An OST single for the film 'Deadpool & Wolverine', showcasing Stray Kids' contribution to international soundtracks.

'NIGHT' and 'Falling Up' OCTOBER 2024
Pre-release OST singles for the anime 'Tower of God: Workshop Battle', available in Korean and English versions.

Come Play OCTOBER 2024
An OST single for 'Arcane Season 2', further cementing Stray Kids' presence in global media.

Japanese Releases

SKZ2020 MARCH 18 2020

ALL IN NOVEMBER 4 2020
Title track 'ALL IN'.

Scars/Thunderous (Japanese Version)
OCTOBER 13 2021

Circus JUNE 22 2022

Other Notable Projects

STEP OUT Series:
Annual video content teasing upcoming releases and activities.

SKZ–RECORD and SKZ–PLAYER:
Special tracks released on YouTube and SoundCloud, showcasing members' individual talents and experiments.

Stray Kids perform at the 2024 Billboard Music Awards

Getting to Know... HAN

STRAY KIDS *Pure Magic*

"There's no need to be perfect. Imperfections make you unique"

Han Ji-sung, known simply as Han, is one of Stray Kids' lead rappers. His ability to deliver complex verses with speed, clarity, and emotion has made him a standout performer, not just within Stray Kids, but in the broader K-pop industry. Also a strong vocalist, his talent and versatility enable him to switch seamlessly between singing and rapping, adding depth and texture to the band's compositions. As part of the production sub-unit 3RACHA, Han has always been deeply involved in the creation of Stray Kids' music. He writes lyrics, composes, and produces tracks. His influences include Eminem, South Korean R&B singer-songwriter Dean, and J.Cole's introspective and socially conscious lyrics. Han's personal experiences and creativity also influence the themes and emotions in Stray Kids' songs. On stage and in videos, Han is known for his high-energy performances. His innate charisma captivates audiences worldwide.

Han live on stage at the American Music Awards 50th Anniversary in Los Angeles, 2024

Born in Incheon, South Korea, on September 14 2000, from a young age, Han displayed a knack for self-expression, often filling his notebooks with doodles, stories, and lyrics – an indication of the multifaceted artist he would become. As a child he was encouraged to explore his interests, and his family often remarked on his ability to find humour in any situation. Han's love for music grew organically. He experimented with different instruments but found his true calling in lyricism and rap. By the time he entered his teenage years, he was writing songs that reflected the two predominant elements of his personality – both the introspective and playful sides. Time spent in Malaysia enabled him to further hone his skills, and on returning to South Korea, he was scouted by JYP Entertainment and auditioned successfully in 2015. Joining the competitive world of JYP trainees, the challenges Han faced during the three years of his training tested his resilience, but he soon stood out for his versatility. Whether it was rapping, singing, or producing, Han's talents were plain to see. He soon became a core member of 3RACHA, alongside Bang Chan and Changbin. Together, they honed their talents, creating original music that would go on to define Stray Kids' distinctive sound. As the group's primary lyricist, Han often explores themes of self-doubt, ambition, and identity which resonate deeply with listeners. Simultaneously, his playful and energetic spirit brings balance to the group dynamic.

Han attends the press conference for Stray Kids' new mini album 樂-STAR (Rock-Star) in Seoul, 2023

FUN FACT FILE

SK He's nicknamed 'Squirrel' among fans for his lively and endearing personality.

SK He adores cheesecake, saying he could eat it every day and would even live in a house made of cheesecake if he could.

SK He is brilliant at impressions and loves mimicking cartoon characters like Doraemon, or other K-pop idols, especially his fellow Stray Kids members.

SK He says his English name is Peter Han.

SK His star sign is Virgo.

When Stray Kids officially debuted in 2018, Han's star quality was impossible to ignore. On stage, he was a powerhouse, seamlessly switching between rapid-fire rap verses and heartfelt vocal lines. His ability to convey raw emotion through his performances earned him widespread acclaim. As a producer, Han has been instrumental in crafting Stray Kids' unique sound. His creative input is a driving force behind the group's success, blending genres and pushing boundaries to deliver a unique musical experiences. Despite his achievements, Han remains grounded, often expressing gratitude to his fans for their love and support.

Offstage, Han is at the very heart of Stray Kids – famous for his quick wit, infectious laughter, and genuine interactions with fans. He is an avid learner and storyteller. Whether it's through sharing anecdotes during live broadcasts or creating comedic skits, he constantly finds ways to connect with his audience – the fact that he's fluent in English, which he learned while living in Malaysia, aids his ability to communicate. His knack of balancing vulnerability with humour makes him one of the most relatable figures in the industry, and fans often describe him as someone who brightens their days.

Sartorially speaking, Han often combines casual streetwear with edgy elements, such as distressed jeans, oversized tops, graphic hoodies, and sneakers. He also likes to incorporate bold prints, colourful beanies, and quirky accessories into his outfits. On stage, his looks range from grunge-inspired to avant-garde. Han is known for experimenting with his hair, sporting everything from natural dark shades to eye-catching colours like platinum blonde or vibrant red. His hairstyles range from messy and effortless to sleek and polished, depending on the concept. While he keeps things natural offstage, on stage he uses make-up to enhance his gorgeous almond-shaped eyes.

Getting to Know HAN

ON THE ROAD

Stray Kids' major concert tours and festival gigs to date…

Performing live in concert during I-Days Milano Coca-Cola at Ippodromo La Maura in Milan, 2024

ON THE ROAD Stray Kids' major concert tours and festival gigs to date...

85

TOURS

Unveil Tour 'I AM...'

January–September 2019

ASIA, AUSTRALIA, EUROPE, AND NORTH AMERICA.

Stray Kids' debut showcase tour, supporting their debut album series 'I Am NOT,' 'I Am WHO,' and 'I Am YOU.'

RANDOM FACT!

Despite its global reach, the tour was not officially labelled as a world tour.

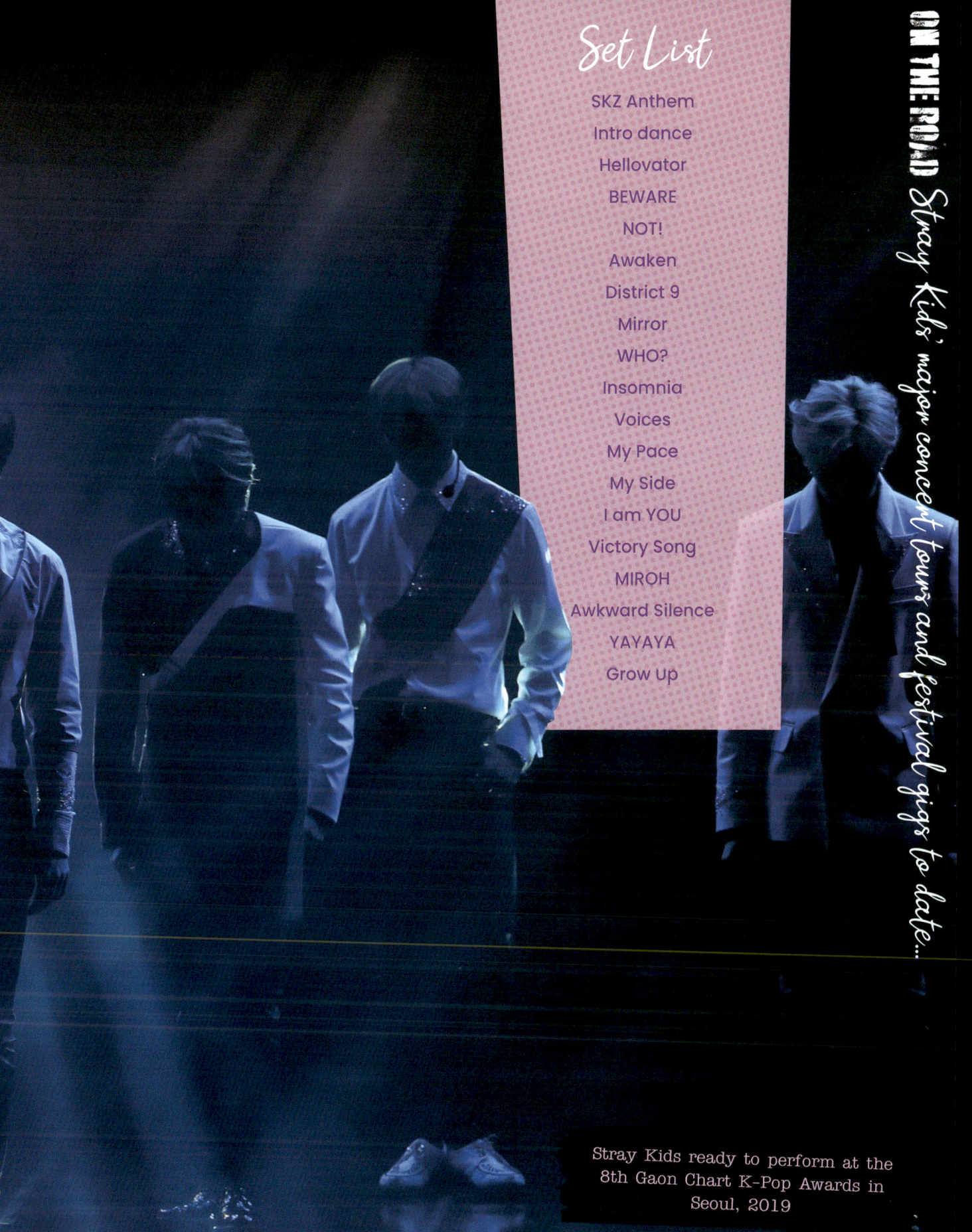

ON THE ROAD — Stray Kids' major concert tours and festival gigs to date...

Set List

SKZ Anthem
Intro dance
Hellovator
BEWARE
NOT!
Awaken
District 9
Mirror
WHO?
Insomnia
Voices
My Pace
My Side
I am YOU
Victory Song
MIROH
Awkward Silence
YAYAYA
Grow Up

Stray Kids ready to perform at the 8th Gaon Chart K-Pop Awards in Seoul, 2019

District 9: Unlock World Tour

November 2019–February 2020
ASIA, NORTH AMERICA AND EUROPE

The tour supported Stray Kids' album *Clé: LEVANTER*. It began in November 2019, but was interrupted by the COVID-19 pandemic.

RANDOM FACT!

At their New York gig, Hyunjin pretended to playfully push Seungmin towards the audience.

ON THE ROAD — *Stray Kids' major concert tours and festival gigs to date...*

Set List

Intro + District 9	19
Victory Song	Get Cool
Question	M.I.A
Rock	Awkward Silence
Side Effects	Astronaut
My Pace	Double Knot
Voices	Levanter
Hellevator	Mixtape #1
Mirror	Grow Up
Chronosaurus	YAYAYA

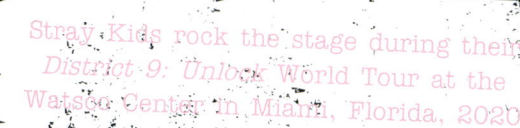

Stray Kids rock the stage during their *District 9: Unlock* World Tour at the Watsco Center in Miami, Florida, 2020

Maniac World Tour

April 2022–April 2023

ASIA, NORTH AMERICA, EUROPE, AND AUSTRALIA

The first world tour after the pandemic, supporting Stray Kids' *ODDINARY* album and other releases. The tour featured multiple sold-out dates and venue upgrades due to high demand.

RANDOM FACT!

The concerts on May 1 2022 in Seoul and July 27 2022 in Tokyo were livestreamed on Beyond LIVE, allowing fans worldwide to participate virtually.

Stray Kids perform at K-Pop Super Live to kick off Seoul Festa 2022 in Seoul

ON THE ROAD *Stray Kids' major concert tours and festival gigs to date...*

Set List

Maniac
VENOM
Red Lights
Easy
All In
District 9
Back Door
Charmer
Lonely St
Side Effects
Thunderous
DOMINO
Star Lost
MIROH
Haven
Grow Up
God's Menu
Hellevator
Top
Victory Song
Surfin'
Domino

5-Star Dome Tour

August–October 2023
JAPAN AND SOUTH KOREA

The 5-Star Dome Tour was Stray Kids' first all-dome tour, supporting their third studio album *5-Star*. The concerts showcased solo performances by individual members, featuring unreleased tracks and special stages. The tour attracted a total of 341,000 attendees in Japan, marking a significant milestone in Stray Kids' career.

Stray Kids take the stage at the 2023 Billboard Music Awards at Hwajung Gymnasium in Seoul

Set List Overview

The setlist for the 5-Star Dome Tour featured a dynamic mix of Stray Kids' popular tracks, including both Korean and Japanese releases. While the exact setlist varied by location, performances typically included...

God's Menu (Japanese Ver.)
All In
Wolfgang
MIROH
CASE 143 (Japanese Ver.)
S-Class (Rock Ver.)
Super Bowl (Japanese Ver.)
Social Path
DOMINO

ON THE ROAD *Stray Kids' major concert tours and festival gigs to date...*

RANDOM FACT!

The demand for tickets was extraordinary, with general sales selling out within five minutes and over 2.5 million applications submitted, reflecting the group's growing popularity.

DominATE World Tour

August 2024 – July 2025
ASIA, NORTH AMERICA, EUROPE, AUSTRALIA, AND LATIN AMERICA

Their biggest tour to date, showcasing Stray Kids' growth as global artists and supporting their latest releases – the Korean EP ATE, the Japanese album *GIANT*, and the mixtape HOP.

This tour has included their first performances at major outdoor stadiums across the globe and marked a milestone in attendance records. Spotify has enhanced the tour experience by setting up interactive booths at venues like the KSPO Dome in Seoul, offering photo zones and exclusive merchandise.

RANDOM FACT!

At the Singapore gig, the group engaged in playful water gun fights on stage, surprising and delighting the audience.

Live on stage at the American Music Awards 50th Anniversary in Los Angeles, 2024

Set List

SKZ Anthem
MOUNTAINS
Thunderous
JJAM
District 9
Back Door
Hold My Hand (Han solo)
Youth (Lee Know solo)
As We Are (Seungmin solo)
So Good (Hyunjin solo)
Chk Chk Boom
TOPLINE
Super Bowl (Japanese version)
COMFLEX
LALALALA
GIANT
Twilight
Lonely St
Social Path
Railway (Bang Chan solo)
HALLUCINATION (I.N solo)
Unfair (Felix solo)
ULTRA (Changbin solo)
GET LIT
ITEM, DOMINO
God's Menu
S-Class
VENOM
MANIAC
I Like It
CASE 143
My Pace
Stray Kids
MIROH
Chk Chk Boom (festival version)

ON THE ROAD Stray Kids' major concert tours and festival gigs to date...

FESTIVALS

Stray Kids perform during Lollapalooza at Grant Park in Chicago, Illinois, 2024

KCON 2018 Japan
Stray Kids made one of their first major international festival appearances in April 2018 at KCON Japan, performing tracks from their debut.

KCON 2018 Los Angeles
They performed in August 2018, marking their U.S. festival debut.

KCON 2019 NY & LA
They returned to KCON in both New York and Los Angeles, delivering energetic performances.

SBS Gayo Daejeon Festivals
Stray Kids are frequent performers at SBS Gayo Daejeon, including their participation in the 2024 Summer Festival in Incheon, where they performed hits like 'Maniac' and 'Chk Chk Boom'.

British Summer Time Hyde Park JULY 14 2024
Stray Kids headlined this prestigious London festival, delivering a high-energy set with songs like 'S-Class', 'Freeze', and 'God's Menu'. This appearance marked their growing influence in Western markets.

Lollapalooza AUGUST 2 2024
The group performed at Lollapalooza in Chicago, showcasing their hit tracks, including 'Thunderous', 'Topline', and 'Super Bowl'.

Asia Song Festival
Stray Kids have participated several times in the Asia Song Festival, an event that brings together top artists from across Asia.

HallyuPopFest 2019, 2022
Featured as headliners, showcasing their music to fans in Southeast Asia.

Korea Times Music Festival 2019
Held in Los Angeles, this festival served as a significant platform for their U.S. audience.

ON THE ROAD Stray Kids' major concert tours and festival gigs to date...

Stray Kids in formation during Lollapalooza at Grant Park in Chicago, Illinois, 2024

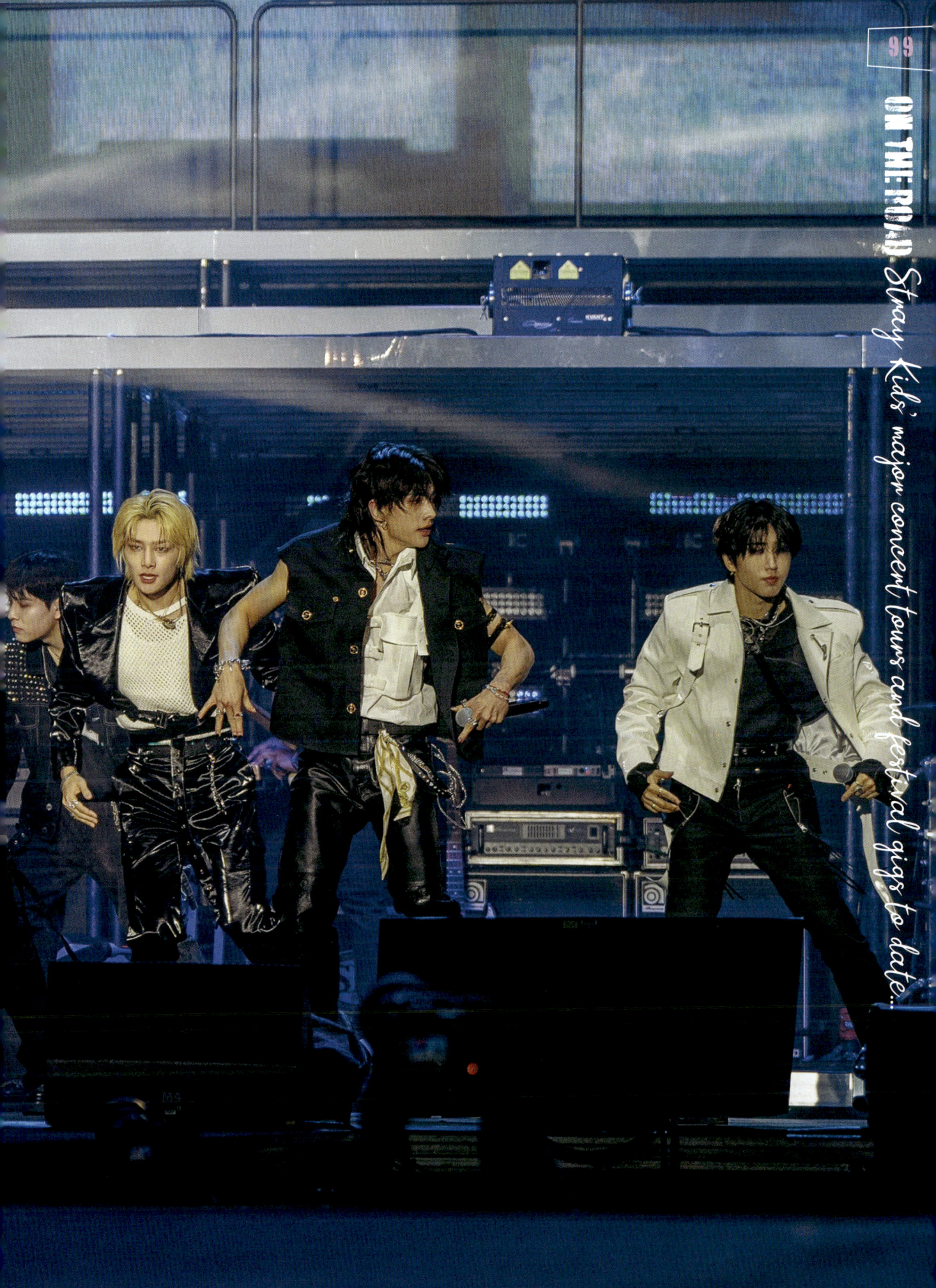

ON THE ROAD — Stray Kids' major concert tours and festival gigs to date...

Getting to Know... FELIX

STRAY KIDS — Pure Magic

"Every little step counts, even if it's small. Progress is progress"

Felix's unique voice is his calling card. It's a deep, rich, velvety tone that adds drama to Stray Kids' songs. In tracks like 'God's Menu', his lines are often the most quoted and replayed – 'Cookin' like a chef, I'm a 5-star Michelin'. Fans are fascinated by the juxtaposition of his voice and angelic appearance. He is also one of the main dancers in the group, often praised for his fluid yet precise moves. But Felix doesn't just rap and dance, he tells stories. Every movement, every word, conveys emotion – whether that be on stage or when messaging fans.

Felix on stage at I-Days Festival, Ippodromo SNAI La Maura, Milan, 2024

Born Lee Yong-bok in Sydney, Australia on September 15 2000, Felix – as he became known – grew up in a multicultural household alongside his two sisters. Life in Oz was a combination of academic pursuits, discovering his love for the arts, and taekwondo lessons – his black belt in the martial art proving his discipline and determination from a young age. He was also a natural dancer with an ability to move to the beat of any song. It was this talent that led him, in 2017, to audition for JYP Entertainment in Australia. With his striking looks, hypnotic dance moves, and that unforgettable voice, he impressed the judges and earned his ticket to South Korea. He was thrilled to move to Seoul, but adapting to life there wasn't easy. He was homesick for his family and his country of birth. Then there were the cultural barriers to navigate, the pressure of a gruelling trainee schedule, and the daunting task of mastering the Korean language. Yet Felix embraced every challenge head-on with resilience becoming one of his defining traits.

FUN FACT FILE

- **SK** His passion for baking has earned him the nicknames 'Cookie Boy' and 'Brownie Boy'.
- **SK** He is a big fan of Anime – his favourites include 'One Piece' and 'Attack on Titan'.
- **SK** His favourite colour is black.
- **SK** He adores cats and is forever expressing his love for them. Fans often imagine him as a cat himself due to his playful and endearing personality.
- **SK** His star sign is Virgo.

In late 2017, Felix joined Stray Kids as a trainee, bringing his unique flair and talents to the competition. But halfway through the show, he faced elimination – a moment that shook him to the core and tested his resolve. Fans were devastated, but happily his skills and perseverance earned him a second chance. Reinstated into the line-up, Felix became an official member of Stray Kids, debuting in March 2018 with the album *I Am NOT* and its powerful title track, 'District 9'. Since then, Felix's distinctive voice, exceptional dance ability, striking visuals, and stage presence have made him an integral member of Stray Kids. Off stage, softly-spoken, freckle-faced Felix is a ray of sunshine with his fellow members describing him as warm, caring, kind and endlessly supportive. Fans know him for his radiant smile, his love of baking (especially brownies!), and his fondness for Anime. Despite his fame, Felix remains down to earth, regularly sharing heartfelt messages of gratitude to fans. Australian by birth and with English as his mother tongue, Felix is a bridge between cultures, representing Stray Kids on the global stage with his understanding of international audiences. He's not just an idol, but a role model for millions.

Felix has a distinctive look. For the everyday, he's often seen in comfy oversized clothing like hoodies, sweaters, and jogging bottoms while frequently incorporating streetwear elements like baggy jeans and graphic T-shirts. Even in casual settings, Felix adds a touch of individuality with unique prints, asymmetrical cuts, and quirky accessories. He loves his chunky chains, earrings, and rings, and has an impressive collection of hats. He dials up somewhat for performances – embracing leather, ripped denim, and dramatic coats. Felix likes to blur traditional gender norms with his style, confidently rocking traditionally female wear such as cropped tops. The boy is bold, and while he favours mostly neutral shades, pops of neon are not unusual. Felix is known for his hair transformations – from fiery reds to icy blondes and back to darker hues, his locks often complement his outfit. Ditto make-up, which he likes to tailor to the occasion. For everyday looks, it's minimal and natural, but for performances, it includes smoky eyes, glitter, and bold eyeliner to emphasize his aquiline features.

Felix attends the Tommy Hilfiger fashion show during New York Fashion Week in New York City, 2024

AWARDS
And the award goes to...

Since debuting in 2018, the Stray Kids have amassed a massive treasure trove of awards.

Stray Kids grace the red carpet at the Asia Artist Awards in Seoul, 2021

Asia Artist Awards

Performance of the Year 2021

Album of the Year for 'MAXIDENT' 2022

Stage of the Year 2023

Hanteo Music Awards

Best Performance 2023

Best Performance 2024

Asia Star Entertainer Awards

Grand Prize 2024

Korean Music Awards – Golden Disc Awards

Best New Artist 2019

Best Performance 2021

Best Album (Bonsang) for 'NOEASY' 2022

Best Album (Bonsang) for 'MAXIDENT' 2023

Most Popular Artist 2023

Best Album (Bonsang) for '★★★★★ (5-STAR)' 2024

Global K-Pop Artist 2024

Stray Kids pose at the Seoul Music Awards in Seoul, 2019

Seoul Music Awards

Rookie of the Year 2019

Main Award (Bonsang) 2021, 2022, 2023, 2024

Circle Chart Music Awards
(formerly Gaon Chart Music Awards)

New Artist of the Year 2019

World Rookie of the Year 2020

The Hot Performance of This Year 2021

World K-pop Star 2022

Artist of the Year – Physical Album (4th Quarter) for 'MAXIDENT' 2023

Artist of the Year – Album for '★★★★★ (5-STAR)' 2024

Mnet Asian Music Awards (MAMA)

Best New Male Artist 2018

Worldwide Fans' Choice Top 10 2021, 2022

Yogibo Chill Artist 2022

The Most Popular Group 2022

Worldwide Fans' Choice 2023

Fans' Choice Male Top 10 2024

The Fact Music Awards

Next Leader 2018

Year Dance Performer 2019

Global Hottest Award 2020

Artist of the Year (Bonsang) 2021, 2022, 2023

Fan N Star Four Star Award 2022, 2023, 2024

MTV Europe Music Awards
Best Korean Act 2020

MTV Video Music Awards
Best K-pop for 'S-Class' 2023

MTV Video Music Awards Japan
Best Group Video (International) for 'CASE 143' 2023

Awards

And the award goes to...

Billboard Music Awards
Top K-pop Album for '★★★★★ (5-STAR)' 2023

iHeartRadio Music Awards
K-pop Album of the Year for '★★★★★ (5-STAR)' 2024

Nickelodeon Mexico Kids' Choice Awards
Favourite K-Pop Group 2023

People's Choice Awards
Group/Duo of the Year 2024

Stray Kids dressed to impress at the 2023 MTV Video Music Awards, New Jersey, 2023

Getting to Know... SEUNGMIN

STRAY KIDS Pure Magic

"STAY, your love and support inspire me to work harder every day"

Kim Seungmin, known simply as Seungmin, is a multifaceted artist whose talents, demeanour, and laid-back personality have captured the hearts of fans worldwide. Not for nothing is he known as the 'gentleman' of the group. As the main vocalist of Stray Kids, Seungmin's smooth, emotive, and technically precise voice is a defining element of the group's sound. His ability to convey deep emotions through his singing adds layers of meaning to the group's diverse discography. From high-energy anthems to heartfelt ballads, Seungmin consistently delivers performances that resonate with fans. Notably, he excels in live settings, showcasing his vocal control even during demanding choreography.

Seungmin on stage at the 2024 Billboard Music Awards

Born on September 22 2000 in Seoul, South Korea, as a child Seungmin was thoughtful and hard-working, excelling in both academic and sporting arenas. However, he also showed a natural inclination towards music and performance which culminated in him auditioning for JYP Entertainment in 2017. His talent and potential was evident from the start as he secured second place in the open auditions. During his trainee years, Seungmin became well-known for his disciplined work ethic, impeccable vocals, and keen attention to detail. These qualities earned him a place in Stray Kids. Seungmin officially debuted with the group in March 2018, and quickly made a name for himself as an exceptional vocalist, his voice combining clarity, versatility, and emotional depth.

Having lived in Los Angeles for a while when he was a child, Seungmin is fluent in English – a skill that enhances Stray Kids' ability to connect with their global fanbase. His language proficiency, combined with his articulate and warm manner often makes him the group's spokesperson on the international stage. Seungmin is admired for his polite and approachable personality, but he also has a sharp wit and playful sense of humour that endears him to both his bandmates and fans. It's true to say that he is a STAY favourite, often engaging with fans through social media and live streams. He has a unique ability to make them feel seen and appreciated. Despite his success, Seungmin remains humble and he's uber focused on self-improvement. His commitment to his craft and his role in Stray Kids has solidified his place as an indispensable member of the group. With his unique combination of talent, charisma, charm, and dedication, Seungmin truly is a gentleman.

Seungmin poses at the TASAKI 70th Anniversary "Floating Shell" pop-up store in Seoul, 2024

Style-wise Seungmin's look reflects his personality – clean, comfortable, and understatedly elegant. Off stage, he favours cozy, oversized sweaters – giving him a boy-next-door vibe. He also rocks a cool preppy look on occasion. Seungmin leans toward neutral colours like beige, white, grey, and soft pastels – shades that reflect his calm personality. He likes to look co-ordinated. For performances, Seungmin adopts more dramatic looks with bold outfits, accessories, and statement pieces to match Stray Kids' high-energy concepts. Even on stage, he retains an aura of co-ordinated style. Seungmin's hairstyle is typically neat and understated, matching his overall look. Colour-wise, he sticks to darker tones, although he occasionally experiments with lighter shades. Seungmin is often described as having 'puppy-like' visuals, but despite his sweet appearance, he can also pull off a more mature and charismatic vibe when required, particularly during performances.

FUN FACT FILE

- **SK** Fans and members often call him 'Snail' due to his adorable, calm demeanour or 'Seungmo'.
- **SK** A passionate baseball enthusiast, he's a loyal fan of the Doosan Bears and had aspirations to become a baseball player before becoming an K-pop idol.
- **SK** He's known for being the group's 'early bird', often waking up before everyone else.
- **SK** He has confessed that he likes sleeping on the edge of his bed instead of the centre.
- **SK** His star sign is Virgo.

WORDS OF WISDOM

Stray Kids are a never-ending source of inspiration

SEUNGMIN

> "No matter how small it seems, every effort you make matters. Be proud of yourself."

> "You're not alone. There are people who care about you and want to see you happy."

> "Mistakes are part of learning. Don't be too hard on yourself – keep moving forward."

> "I don't believe in forevers, but in this moment, I want to believe in eternity with you."

> "If you focus on the hurt, you will continue to suffer but, if you focus on the lesson, you will continue to grow."

WORDS OF WISDOM

STRAY KIDS *Pure Magic*

BANG CHAN

> "It's okay to take your time. Everyone grows at their own pace."

> "It's really important to show the world who you are and express yourself because it's not like everyone's going to be like, "Oh, back away". There will be some people who open up and accept you as well."

> "Well, I'm pretty sure, whatever you're doing, whether it's school, whether it's work, whether it's something that is very artistic or whether it is something that is very business-wise, whether it is games, whether it's playing sports. . . Whatever it is, I'm pretty sure you're doing a good job."

> "Always be kind to yourself. You deserve love and care from the most important person in your life - you."

> "It's okay to cry. It's okay to feel weak. But don't forget that you're capable of overcoming anything."

STRAY KIDS *Pure Magic*

HYUNJIN

> "I hope people who can't express themselves freely with words, can express themselves through something else like writing, drawing, or anything you like."

> "If you are happy now, just enjoy being happy now. You don't have to worry about bad things. It feels like a waste of that happiness."

> "You're not alone. No matter how far apart we are, my heart is always with you."

> "You don't have to be perfect to be loved. You're loved just as you are."

> "The hard times will pass. Just hold on a little longer, and you'll see brighter days."

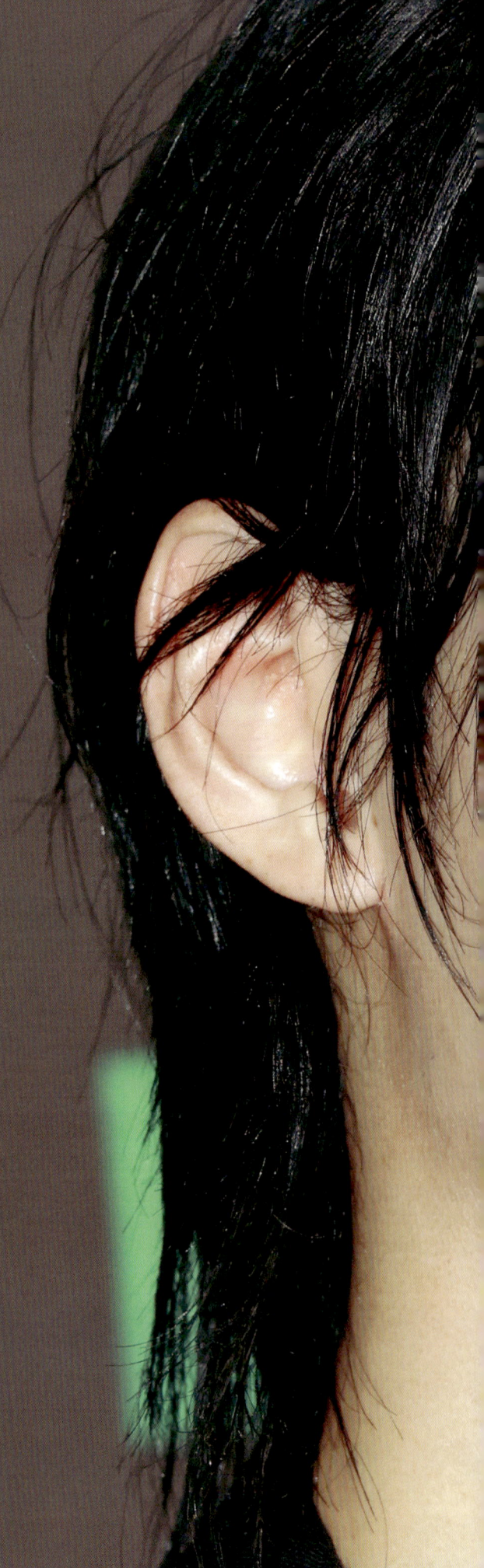

FELIX

> "Be happy and make sure you focus on positive aspects in life and go for what you love."

> "Go at your own pace, and we'll rise to the top as one."

> "No matter what, I believe in you. You're stronger than you think."

> "Every day is a new opportunity to grow. Be proud of every step you take."

> "You're not alone, no matter how far apart we are. I'm always cheering for you."

LEE KNOW

› "Let go of what you had, cherish what you have, and search for what you want."

› "Don't close your eyes. Have some courage and there will be light somewhere."

› "You don't need to compare yourself to others. Your journey is unique."

› "You're allowed to make mistakes. That's how you learn and grow stronger."

› "Even if you feel like giving up, don't. Because giving up means you're giving up on yourself."

HAN

> "There must be gloominess for one to see the light. If there's light you wouldn't know whether you're happy or not."

> "Anyone can be anything, you can be everything."

> "Don't be afraid to be yourself. Your uniqueness is your greatest strength."

> "Take life one step at a time. There's no need to rush. Enjoy the moments."

> "No matter how hard it gets, remember that you're strong enough to overcome it."

STRAY KIDS Pure Magic

I.N

> "Don't compare your life to others. There's no comparison between the sun and the moon. They both shine at their own times."

> "Our greatest weakness lies in giving up. The most certain way to succeed is always to try one more time."

> "It's okay to take your time. Everyone's journey is different, and that's what makes it special."

> "Don't be afraid to make mistakes. They're proof that you're trying and learning."

> "No matter how hard things get, there's always a way forward. Keep going, and you'll find it."

CHANGBIN

> "In the middle of a lonely night, I try my best to smile brightly just like the street lights."

> "When it feels like no one understands, remember that you're not alone. You have us."

> "Your happiness matters. Don't be afraid to prioritize yourself sometimes."

> "It's okay to take small steps. What matters is that you're moving forward."

> "Dreams don't become reality by magic; they come true through hard work and determination."

Getting to Know...

I.N

"The members are like my family. I couldn't do this without them"

STRAY KIDS *Pure Magic*

130

As the maknae (youngest member) of Stray Kids, I.N plays a vital role in the dynamics of the group. While often considered the group's adorable baby brother, he has proven himself to be more than just a source of cuteness. His vocals have greatly improved since the group's debut in 2018, allowing him to tackle complex melodies and emotionally charged lines with confidence. While I.N is primarily known for his warm vocals and cheeky personality, his journey as a dancer is equally noteworthy. This growth is evident in the wide range of choreography he performs – from hard-hitting, intense tracks like 'God's Menu' and 'Thunderous', to more fluid, emotive performances in 'Astronaut' and 'Grow Up'. I.N skilfully adapts his movements to the mood and energy of each song. His dedication to his craft and his perseverance are truly awesome.

I.N performs for I-Days at Ippodromo SNAI La Maura in Milan, 2024

Yang Jeongin, known to fans as I.N, was born on February 8, 2001, in Busan, South Korea. His musical journey began with dreams of becoming a singer. Before his K-pop career, he trained for two years in traditional Korean music, focusing on 'pansori' – a genre of narrative singing that requires immense vocal strength and emotion. This foundation is evident in the depth and stability of his vocals, which have become a signature aspect of Stray Kids' sound. When I.N first appeared on Stray Kids, the JYP survival show in 2017 having been a trainee for two years – he admitted that dancing was not his strongest skill, having had limited experience of contemporary dance styles. However, he tackled this challenge head-on, working tirelessly alongside his members to improve his technique and synchronization. Learning from those more experienced in dance such as Lee Know and Hyunjin, I.N absorbed their feedback and training, and often credits his 'hyungs' or elders for their guidance and patience. I.N's initial struggles only fuelled his determination to match the high standard of performance expected and over time, I.N not only caught up to his peers but also began to shine in his own right. What sets I.N apart is his expression. His ability to combine technical execution with emotional depth allows him to bring a sense of the unique to every performance. Whether it's the precise, sharp movements of a powerful anthem or the smooth, flowing gestures of a heartfelt ballad, I.N consistently conveys his intended emotions with authenticity.

I.N poses at the Alexander McQueen SS24 show during Paris Fashion Week in Paris, 2023

Optimistic, resilient, and ever-smiling, I.N lifts up his bandmates when times get tough. He instinctively knows when to crack a cheeky joke or slip in words of positivity to lighten the mood. His look reflects these positive personality traits – think youthful optimism and casual chic tempered with sophisticated vibes in neutral shades. Oversized hoodies, loose-fitting shirts, sweaters, and baggy jeans. For a more formal feel, I.N rocks a tailored blazer. On stage, like all the Stray Kids, he goes bold – with edgy streetwear, leather jackets, and crazily-patterned shirts. I.N doesn't do subtle when it comes to his hair. He's known for experimenting with colour – from natural black to lighter blonde shades – even pastels. Styles range from soft and natural waves to sleek looks for performances. Make-up wise, he's minimal when not performing, but glows up for the stage, using sharp eyeliner to enhance those doe-like eyes.

FUN FACT FILE

- **SK** Fans and members call him 'Desert Fox' because of his resemblance to the animal, and 'Baby Bread' due to his adorable appearance. He's also affectionately known as 'Innie'.

- **SK** Having debuted wearing braces on his teeth, I.N has become a braces icon with fans feeling it added to his innate cuteness. He's since had them removed, and revels in showing off his perfect smile.

- **SK** He has a small scar on his arm that he got from an accident during childhood.

- **SK** During the *Stray Kids* idol show, I.N accidentally wore mismatched socks, which became a running joke among fans.

- **SK** His star sign is Aquarius.

Stray Kids...
THE FUTURE

Looking forwards, Stray Kids' evolution promises to be as dynamic and impactful as their rise to prominence. Here are some predictions...

Stray Kids have always been synonymous with innovation, so it's likely their sound will grow even more experimental, blending elements of global music trends with their signature high-energy style. The group's members, in particular 3RACHA, will continue to pioneer self-produced tracks that push the boundaries of what K-pop can achieve. Themes will delve into deeper societal issues, personal growth, and universal struggles, fostering even stronger emotional connections with their music. Collaborative projects with international artists – spanning genres like hip-hop, EDM, and alternative pop – will further cement their place as global trailblazers.

Stray Kids... THE FUTURE

Stray Kids perform during Lollapalooza at Grant Park in Chicago, Illinois, 2024

The future will see Stray Kids moving beyond K-pop to dominate the world. Their presence in Western markets, particularly the United States and Europe, will grow stronger, with more extensive world tours and festival appearances. Headlining major events like Coachella or Glastonbury is not just a dream, but a likely reality, showcasing their ability to captivate diverse audiences. The group's influence could also expand into unexpected areas. Imagine Stray Kids lending their voices to a global anthem or being featured in international campaigns advocating for youth empowerment, mental health awareness, or climate change – issues that resonate with their values and their fans.

Looking ahead, Stray Kids will also be defined by their embrace of technology. Virtual reality concerts and augmented reality experiences could transform how they connect with fans. The group may become pioneers in the metaverse, creating immersive fan events that allow STAYs to interact with them in a digital space, breaking the boundaries of physical distance.

Stray Kids in concert at the La Maura Hippodrome in Milan 2024

Interactive apps and AI-driven music platforms could allow fans to remix Stray Kids' tracks, creating a participatory culture where fans and artists collaborate. Their innovative use of social media will continue to set new standards, blending authenticity with cutting-edge digital strategies.

While the group's collective strength remains their core, each member will likely explore individual passions that add depth to Stray Kids' legacy. Hyunjin's artistry could lead him to pursue exhibitions and collaborations in the art world, while Felix's charm and bilingual skills might make him a global ambassador for major brands or an actor in international films.

Changbin's lyrical prowess might result in solo rap albums, and Han's diverse talents could span both music and literature. Seungmin's and I.N's vocal strengths might lead them to pursue solo projects. As a group, these ventures would showcase their versatility while keeping their bond intact.

Stray Kids and their fandom, STAY, share a relationship built on mutual trust and love. This bond will only strengthen over time, with the group continually finding ways to involve STAY in their journey. From exclusive fan events to meaningful projects that give back to the community, Stray Kids will ensure that their fans remain at the heart of everything they do.

The group's ability to create safe spaces through their music and interactions will solidify their position as role models. Their influence will inspire a new generation of artists and fans alike to pursue authenticity and resilience.

As Stray Kids continue to carve their path, their legacy will redefine what it means to be a K-pop group. They're not just performers; they are storytellers, innovators, and cultural ambassadors. Decades from now, Stray Kids' name will stand as a symbol of perseverance and creativity.

Whether through record-breaking albums, philanthropic efforts, or groundbreaking collaborations, Stray Kids will leave an indelible mark on the world. Their journey is far from over, and their future shines as brightly as the dreams they've inspired in millions.

Stray Kids at the 8th Gaon Chart K-Pop Awards in Seoul, 2019

Stray Kids perform at the 2024 Billboard Music Awards.

141

Stray Kids ... THE FUTURE